S0-EUT-765

Football Legends

by Bob Italia

Published by Abdo & Daughters, 6535 Cecilia Circle, Bloomington, Minnesota 55439

Library bound edition distributed by Rockbottom Books, Pentagon Tower, P.O. Box 36036, Minneapolis, Minnesota 55435

Copyright© 1990 by Abdo Consulting Group, Inc., Pentagon Tower, P.O. Box 36036, Minneapolis, Minnesota 55435. International copyrights reserved in all countries. No part of this book may be reproduced in any form without written permission from the publisher. Printed in the United States.

Library of Congress Number: 90-083606   ISBN: 1-56239-007-4

Cover Photo by: Bettmann Newsphotos

Inside Photos by: Bettmann Newsphotos
Pages: 4, 6, 10, 16, 19, 20, 32, 35, 37, 38, 40, 43, 45, 47

Wide World Photos
Pages: 12, 25

Globe Photos
Page: 24

Vernon J. Bieuer Photo
Page: 30

Edited by Rosemary Wallner

— Contents —

Introduction 5
Butkus 7
The Galloping Ghost 13
Largent 21
Montana 27
Brown 39

Introduction

Of all the major sports, football requires the most strength and endurance. To become a football champion, an athlete must practice hard—and have the determination to be the best. These five professional football players have dominated their positions on the field and have earned their honored place in football history.

*The crowd — the touchdown —
the exciting game of football.*

Butkus

Richard (Dick) Butkus was born December 9, 1942, in Chicago, Illinois. One of nine children, Butkus grew up on Chicago's rough south side. Butkus took a natural interest in football. By the time he was in fifth grade, he had decided he wanted to play in the National Football League (NFL).

Dick Butkus

Butkus went to Chicago's Vocational High School. The football coach at Vocational was Bernie O'Brien, a University of Notre Dame graduate. Butkus thought O'Brien was the best football coach in Chicago. Butkus did not even mind walking the five miles to school. He was glad O'Brien was his coach.

The only sport Butkus played at Vocational was football. He practiced hard during the off-season and did exercises that improved his strength. Butkus became a star fullback and linebacker for Vocational. He became known for his strength and for the force of his tackling. By the end of his senior year, Butkus was named a high school all-American. Every major college in the country wanted Dick Butkus to play football for them.

Butkus chose to attend the University of Illinois because it was close to his home. At first, he had trouble with his studies. His coach, Pete Elliot, helped him develop better study habits. Butkus kept up his grades and continued to play football.

Butkus practiced long, hard hours, leaving him little time to make friends. But because of his determination and hard work, he was an instant star as a center and linebacker with Illinois.

In 1963, Butkus stood six feet three inches and weighed two hundred forty-five pounds. His shoe size was eleven-and-a-half triple E. Twenty-one-year-old Butkus led his team to victory over Michigan State as Illinois clinched the title in the Big Ten Conference. In the Rose Bowl, Butkus played with his usual fierceness as Illinois beat the University of Washington.

Butkus was named a college all-American and Lineman of the Year in 1963 and again in 1964. At the end of his senior year, Butkus finished third in the Heisman Trophy voting (the Heisman Trophy is awarded yearly to the best college player). After he graduated, the Chicago Bears chose Butkus in the first round of the college draft. They signed him to a contract worth an amazing $235,000 a year.

In 1965, Butkus, who wore number 51 and played middle linebacker, intercepted five passes. His ferocious tackling made him a fan favorite. At the end of his rookie season, Butkus was named to the all-NFL team—an honor he would retain for eight straight seasons.

Though Butkus and teammate Gale Sayers became superstars in the sixties, the Chicago Bears never won more than seven games in a season. But Butkus averaged over two hundred tackles per season. By 1971, he had nineteen interceptions and twenty fumble recoveries.

After the 1971 season, Butkus had major knee surgery that slowed him down. Still, in 1972, Butkus broke the NFL record for career fumble recoveries with twenty-four. After playing in pain for another year, Dick Butkus finally retired from football in 1973. In 1979, he was named to the Pro Football Hall of Fame, earning him the title of greatest middle linebacker ever.

Playing linebacker for the Chicago Bears, Butkus averaged over 200 tackles per season.

The Galloping Ghost

Harold (Red) Grange was born June 13, 1903, in Wheaton, Illinois, where his father was chief of police. When he was eight years old, Grange was told by a doctor that he had a heart condition and should not be active. But Grange had a lot of energy and ignored the doctor. He took a strong interest in sandlot football. His heart never gave him problems.

Red Grange – The Galloping Ghost.

By the time he reached high school, Grange was bored with the small-town life in Wheaton. He wanted to quit school and go to the nearby city of Chicago. But his father convinced Grange to stay. To pass the time, Grange decided to play high school sports.

Grange quickly excelled in track and basketball. But football was his favorite sport. During his playing days at Wheaton High School, Grange scored seventy-five touchdowns, averaging five a game. Colleges everywhere wanted Grange. He finally decided to go to the University of Illinois. Grange, along with two hundred other players, tried out for the Illinois freshman team. By the end of the first week, Grange was considered the number one running back.

The following year, 1923, Grange played for the varsity team. In his first college game against the University of Nebraska, Grange had touchdown runs of thirty-five, sixty-five, and twelve yards as Illinois won 24-7. He finished the season with twelve touchdowns in only six games. Grange was a quick, elusive runner. He often frustrated would-be tacklers. The sportswriters began calling him the "Galloping Ghost." (He was also called "Red" because of his wavy red hair.)

The six-foot, one-hundred-eighty-five-pound Grange had become a star in the Big Ten Conference. But other teams in the conference still had their doubts about his playing abilities. In 1924, the Michigan Wolverines came to Illinois for a football game. They were determined to stop Grange whenever he got the ball.

Michigan kicked off. Grange took the ball on the five-yard line and raced ninety-five years for a touchdown. Then, after Michigan was forced to punt, Grange took the ball and ran sixty-seven yards for another score. The fans went wild. But Grange was not through.

After Michigan was forced to punt again, Grange took the ball on the second play from scrimmage and raced fifty-six yards for his third touchdown in less than seven minutes. Michigan was stopped again and was forced to punt. Grange got the ball and ran forty-four yards for a touchdown. Grange had made four touchdowns in the first quarter. The crowd applauded Grange for five minutes.

Red Grange eludes a tackler during a Chicago Bears's training session.

In the second half, Grange scored another touchdown, giving him five for the game. He also rushed for 409 yards in the three quarters he played.

One year later, Grange silenced his critics when he rushed for 363 yards and three touchdowns against mighty Penn State. In his three seasons with Illinois, Grange gained 3,637 yards with a record 31 touchdowns.

On November 21, 1925, the day after his last college game, twenty-two-year-old Grange became a professional football player. He was signed to George Halas's Chicago Bears, a team that was part of the newly established National Football League (NFL). Grange signed for an incredible $100,000 a year. Everyone in America wanted to see the Galloping Ghost play football. Halas knew that Grange's presence on the Bears would help the NFL succeed.

A record crowd of 36,000 people packed Wrigley Field in Chicago to see Grange play in his first professional game. His opponents, the Chicago Cardinals, feared Grange so much they punted the ball away from him. The game ended in a tie, 0-0.

In his next game, however, Grange ran for 140 yards. Over 28,000 people cheered him as the Bears won 14-13. Then the Bears went on an eight-game, twelve-day road trip to capitalize on Grange's popularity. In New York, 72,000 people came to watch the Galloping Ghost and the Bears beat the New York Giants 19-7. That twelve-day road trip made the NFL a success.

In 1927, only two years after he had joined the Bears, Grange popped his knee during a game. Knee surgery would have ended his career, so Grange wore a cast and walked on crutches for almost a year before he could run again. Although he exercised his knee, he was never the same.

Despite his injury, Grange remained one of the NFL's biggest stars throughout the twenties and thirties. As his career neared its end, Grange led the Bears to victory in the NFL's first title play-off game in 1933. Then, after a 230-pound lineman caught Grange from behind in the last game of the 1935 season, thirty-two-year-old Grange decided to retire from football.

Red Grange: one of football's most important legends.

During his entire eighteen-year football career, Grange gained 33,820 yards and averaged 8.4 yards a carry. He was named to the all-NFL team four times. In 1963, he was elected to the Pro Football Hall of Fame. If it hadn't been for Red Grange, the NFL might not be the highly successful sports attraction it is today.

Steve Largent makes one of his incredible catches.

Largent

Stephen (Steve) Largent was born September 28, 1954, in Tulsa, Oklahoma. As a young boy, Largent was small, slow, and shy. His father, Jim Largent, left the family when Steve Largent was six years old. His mother, Sue, remarried an electrician three years later. Largent, his mother, and stepfather moved four times in two years. As a result, Largent never had much of a chance to make friends.

Largent attended Putnam City High School in Oklahoma City. He tried out for halfback on the football team, but the coach thought he was too slow. Then Largent tried out for wide receiver. Still the coach thought Largent was too slow. But Largent was determined to play football. He often dove for passes that were off the mark, catching many of them. His persistence impressed the coach. Eventually, Largent made the team.

Largent received a football scholarship from the University of Tulsa in Oklahoma. Tulsa's coach, Jerry Rhome, liked to use a passing offense, and Largent fit in nicely. In 1974 and 1975, Largent led the nation in touchdown catches with fourteen each year.

But Largent's accomplishments went unnoticed. He was not selected in the college football draft until the fourth round by the Houston Oilers. Largent did not do well with Houston. He felt like he did not fit in, and he had a hard time learning the plays. Houston gave up on Largent and traded him to the Seattle Seahawks before the 1976 season.

Largent's former Tulsa coach, Jerry Rhome, was now Seattle's offensive coach. Largent already understood Rhome's offensive plays and quickly became a starter. Though he was not very big or fast (Largent stood only five feet eleven inches and weighed one hundred ninety pounds), Largent became an excellent wide receiver by using his intelligence. He studied films of opponent's defensive backs. He learned about their weaknesses. During a game, Largent took advantage of those weaknesses through tricks he had learned in college. By the end of his first professional season, Largent had 54 receptions for 705 yards. Then in 1978, Largent led the American Football Conference (AFC) with 71 catches and 1,167 yards—one shy of the league lead. For his efforts, Largent was named to the Pro Bowl (the NFL all-star game).

Largent had one of his best seasons in 1979. He gained 1,237 yards with an average of 19 yards a catch. In the play-offs against the Denver Broncos, the Seahawks were behind 23-21 with two minutes remaining. Largent looked as though he was going to run a short passing route. Suddenly, he got behind the Denver defenders. A pass was thrown to Largent, and he caught it for a long touchdown. Seattle won the play-off game. Seattle did not make it to the Super Bowl, but Largent was named an all-pro for the second straight year.

In 1980, Largent caught 66 passes for 1,064 yards and 6 touchdowns. The next year, he caught 75 passes for 1,224 yards and 9 touchdowns and again was named to the Pro Bowl.

After an off year in 1982, Largent had another fine season in 1983 with 72 catches for 1,074 yards and 11 touchdowns. The Seattle Seahawks made it all the way to the AFC title game, but lost.

From 1984 to 1987, Largent averaged over 50 catches and around 1,000 yards per season. Each of those years, he was named to the all-pro team. In 1987, Largent broke Charlie Joyner's record for most career catches (750).

The records did not stop there. The next year, thirty-four-year-old Largent passed Joyner as the all-time leader in receiving yardage with 12,147. Then in 1989, Largent caught his one hundredth career touchdown (another record). He became the first NFL receiver to amass 13,000 yards.

24

When he retired at the end of the 1989 season, Steve Largent had established records for most career receptions, most career touchdowns, most consecutive games receiving a pass (167), most career yardage, most seasons with 50 or more pass receptions (10), and most seasons with 1,000 yards or more in pass receptions (8).

Montana

Joseph (Joe) Montana, Jr., was born June 11, 1956, in Monongahela, Pennsylvania. His father, Joseph, worked at a finance company. Montana's father was a big football fan. He would often play with Montana when he got home from work. Montana practiced throwing the football through a swinging tire. This helped develop his quarterback skills at an early age.

Joe Montana of the San Francisco 49ers.

Montana first played on an organized football team when he was eight years old. By the time he was in high school, Montana had become an all-American football player. He also was an all-state basketball player. Standing six feet, two inches, Montana could dunk a basketball easily. But Montana, thinking of the future, knew he was not tall enough to play professional basketball. So he gave his full attention to football.

By the time he was a senior, Montana was highly recruited by many colleges. In 1974, Montana chose Notre Dame in Indiana because of its fine football team. The classes at Notre Dame were hard. Montana had to study a lot. On the field, he had to compete against six other quarterbacks who had been recruited.

In 1975, Montana got his first big break. Notre Dame's starting quarterback was injured in the third game of the season. Montana took his place and led Notre Dame to victory. Two games later, Montana again replaced the starting quarterback and won the game with an eighty-yard touchdown pass.

When the 1976 college season began, many people thought twenty-year-old Montana would become Notre Dame's starting quarterback. But Montana separated his shoulder and missed the entire season. By 1977 Montana, now a junior, was the third-string quarterback. In the third game of the season against Purdue University, Montana replaced the first two Notre Dame quarterbacks after they could not break the Purdue defense. Montana rallied Notre Dame to victory and earned the starting quarterback job. Notre Dame did not lose a game for the rest of the season.

In 1979, Montana led Notre Dame to the Cotton Bowl against the University of Houston. Down 34-12 in the third quarter, Notre Dame came back under Montana's direction. Notre Dame won the game with two seconds left as Montana threw an eight-yard touchdown pass. Montana had proven his ability to rally his Notre Dame team time and time again. His rallying ability would make him famous during his professional football career.

Montana's rallying ability has made him famous in the NFL.

After the 1979 Cotton Bowl, Montana moved to Los Angeles and waited to be drafted by an NFL team. Though Montana was confident he could play professional football, he was not drafted until the third round (he was the eighty-second player chosen). He was drafted by the San Francisco 49ers, one of the NFL's worst teams.

But in 1979, the 49ers got a new coach, Bill Walsh. Walsh was patient with Montana and developed him slowly. Montana did not play much that season. The 49ers finished the season with a 2-14 record.

In 1980, Montana was the starting quarterback for the last four games. In a game against New Orleans, Montana rallied the 49ers from a 35-7 deficit to a 38-35 victory. Montana was ready to become the starting quarterback for the entire 1981 season.

That year, Montana led the 49ers to the National Football Conference (NFC) Western Division title. In the NFC championship game against the Dallas Cowboys, the 49ers were down 27-21 with less than five minutes remaining. Montana directed a drive to the Cowboy's six-yard line.

Montana's controlled passing made him a threat to opposing teams' defense.

There were only fifty-eight seconds remaining, and it was third down. Montana dropped back to pass, saw his tight end Dwight Clark along the back of the end zone, and threw a high soft pass in Clark's direction. Clark leaped high and came down with the ball for a touchdown. The 49ers had won. They were headed to their first Super Bowl.

Super Bowl XVI was held in the Silverdome in Pontiac, Michigan. Montana directed the 49ers to a 20-0 halftime lead over the Cincinnati Bengals. The 49ers held on for a 26-21 victory. Joe Montana was named the game's Most Valuable Player (MVP).

The next year was an off year for the 49ers. But in 1983, Montana and the 49ers returned to post-season play and made it all the way to the NFC title game, which they lost 24-21 to the Washington Redskins. In 1984, the 49ers beat the Chicago Bears in the NFC championship game, and found themselves playing the Miami Dolphins and their dazzling quarterback, Dan Marino, in Super Bowl XIX. Montana finished the game with 331 passing yards and three touchdowns as the 49ers won their second Super Bowl. The final score was 38-16. Montana was named MVP. For being the NFC's top-rated passer, Montana was named to the Pro Bowl team.

Montana was named to the Pro Bowl the following season, but the 49ers lost to the New York Giants in the play-offs. Then in 1986, Montana had back surgery early in the season. The doctors feared Montana would never play football again. But Montana was determined to return that season. He worked hard to strengthen himself. By November, thirty-year-old Montana was ready to return to the field. In his first game after the surgery, Montana threw three touchdown passes as the 49ers beat the St. Louis Cardinals 43-17. The 49ers returned to the play-offs again, but were eliminated.

In 1987, the 49ers again made it to the play-offs, and again were eliminated. Because of Montana's recurring back problems, people wondered if Montana was on the decline. In 1988, Montana began sharing the quarterback job with Steve Young, whom Coach Walsh labeled as the 49ers future starting quarterback.

Later in his career, Montana suffered from back injuries.

When the 49ers reached the play-offs, Walsh decided to start Montana because of his experience.

The decision was a wise one. Montana led the 49ers to the Super Bowl. In the game, Montana rallied the 49ers over the Cincinnati Bengals, engineering a last-minute touchdown drive. The 49ers had won their third Super Bowl in as many appearances. Instead of criticizing Montana, sportswriters everywhere said that he was one of the best quarterbacks ever.

In 1989, however, Bill Walsh quit as head coach of the 49ers. Many thought the new coach, George Siefert, could not bring the 49ers back to the Super Bowl. But Montana had his best year ever as he completed more than 70 percent of his passes with 26 touchdowns. And the 14-2 49ers found themselves in the Super Bowl. Montana threw five touchdown passes as the 49ers won 55-10 over the Denver Broncos. Montana was named MVP. Now there was no doubt that Joe Montana was the best quarterback ever.

Joe Montana: the best quarterback ever!

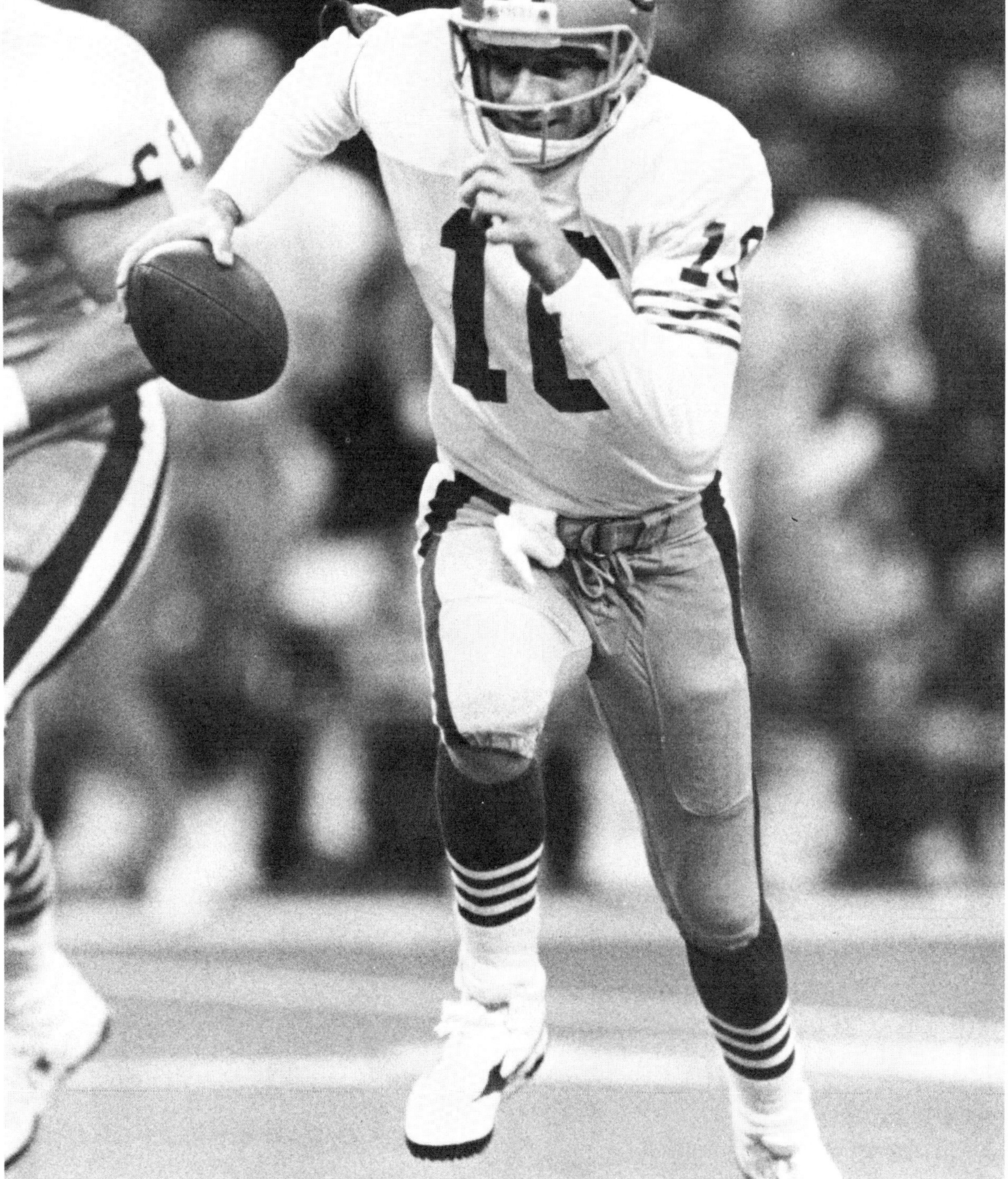

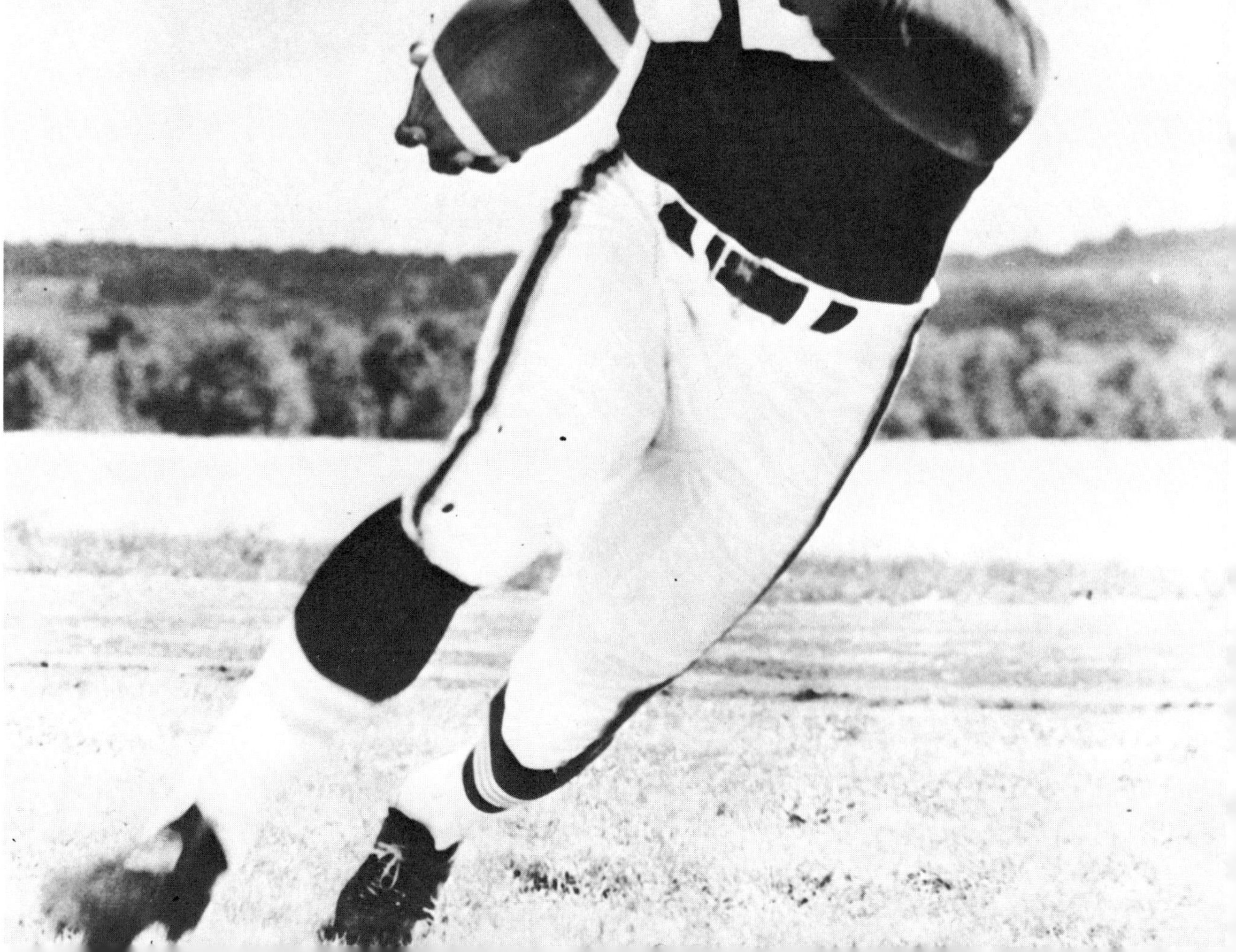

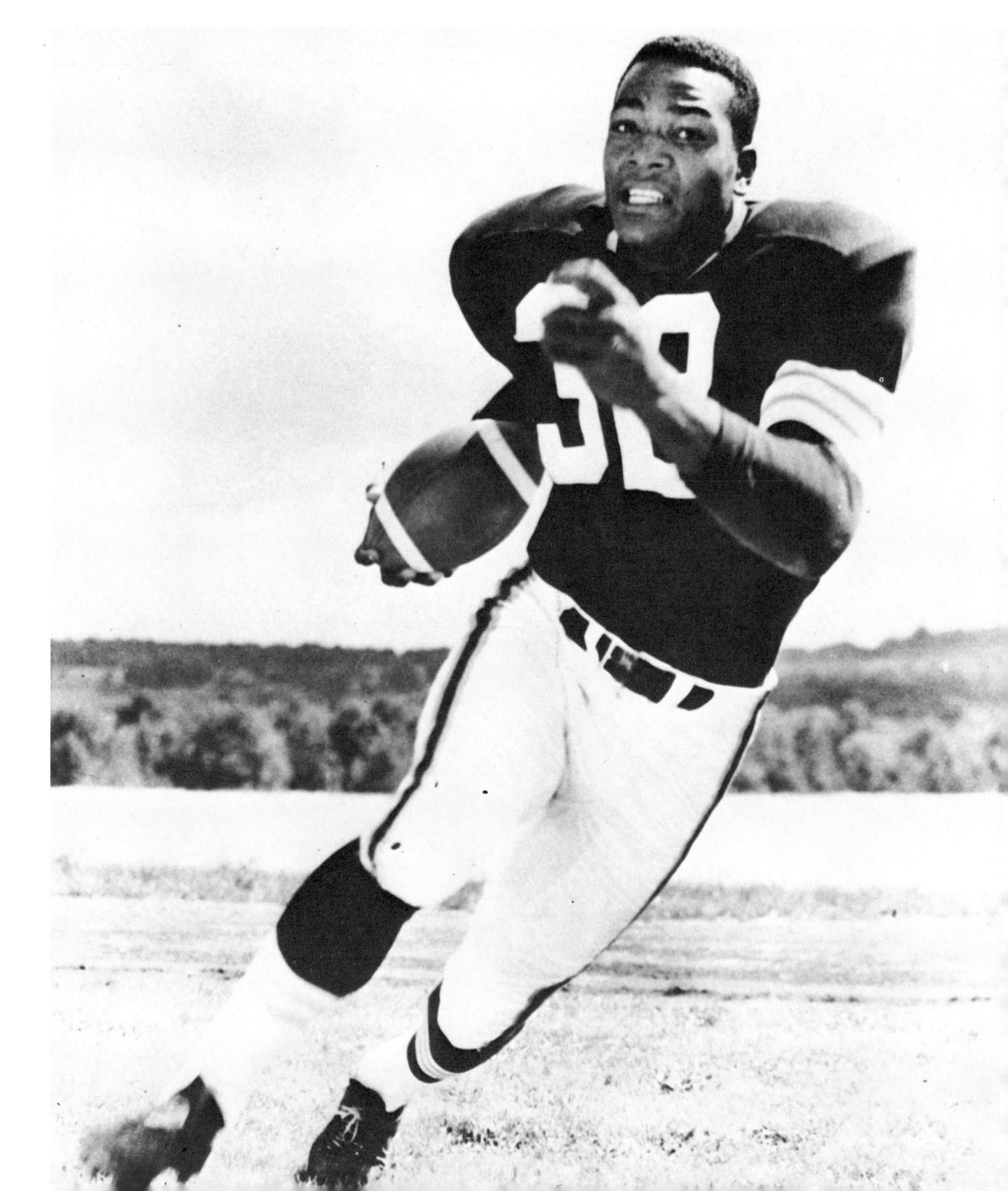

Brown

James (Jim) Brown was born February 17, 1936, on St. Simons Island, Georgia. His father, a gambler called "Sweet Sue," ran away from his family shortly after Brown was born. His mother left soon after that to find work in New York. Brown was left in the care of his great-grandmother. He spent much of his time on the beaches of the island.

Jim Brown: star running back.

Jim Brown was a natural athlete.

When Brown was seven years old, he moved to Manhasset on Long Island, New York. He lived with his mother who worked as a maid. As he grew older, Brown joined a gang, the Gaylords, and soon became their leader. But his love of sports saved him from a life of crime. Those early years playing on the beaches of St. Simons had made Jim Brown a natural athlete. He spent his free time playing as many sports as he could—especially football.

When he enrolled in Manhasset High School, Brown became an instant star athlete. By the time he reached his junior year, Brown stood six feet two inches and weighed one hundred ninety-five pounds. As a halfback, Brown averaged fifteen yards per carry. He was also an excellent blocker and tackler. In basketball, Brown averaged 38.1 points per game, scoring fifty-five points in one game, and making twenty-two of twenty-four free throws in another. In track, Brown won the state high jump crown. He was even considered the best lacrosse player on Long Island. Brown also pitched for the baseball team, and was scouted by the New York Yankees. In all, Brown won thirteen letters in five different sports at Manhasset High. He received forty-two college scholarship offers. Football, however, remained his favorite sport.

Brown chose to attend nearby Syracuse University where he played lacrosse and football. In lacrosse, Brown became an all-American player. But it was football that earned him the greatest attention.

Brown played his first football game as a sophomore. He became a starter on the sixth game of the eight-game season. In that game, Brown had a 54-yard run and totaled 145 yards. He finished the season with 439 yards and a 5.8 yards-per-carry average.

By his senior year, Brown was an all-American football player. He rushed for 986 yards with a 6.2-yard average. He also was the kicker, played defensive back, and returned kickoffs.

In his final Syracuse game, Brown scored forty-three points. In the Cotton Bowl, Brown gained 132 yards rushing and scored 21 points. Brown finished his college career with 2,091 yards rushing with 25 touchdowns. Professional football teams everywhere wanted Jim Brown.

Brown played college football for Syracuse University in New York.

Brown wanted to play for the New York Giants, but he was selected fourth in the college draft by the Cleveland Browns. Brown signed for $15,000 a year. By now, Jim Brown weighed 230 pounds.

Despite his strength and size, Brown became an elusive runner. In college, Brown could run over people. But in professional football, many of the defensive linemen were over 260 pounds.

As a rookie, Brown became an instant star. In one game, Brown ran for 237 yards in 31 carries. At the time, that was a league record. He finished the season with 942 yards (the lowest of his career) and won the rushing title. Then he was named Rookie of the Year and all-pro. And he was only twenty-one years old.

In his second year, Brown, in only five games, set a team record for most touchdowns in a season with fourteen. Brown gained a record 1,527 yards for the season, averaging 5.9 yards a carry and winning the rushing title once again. He was also named the NFL's Most Valuable Player.

In one professional game of his rookie year, Brown ran for 237 yards in 31 carries.

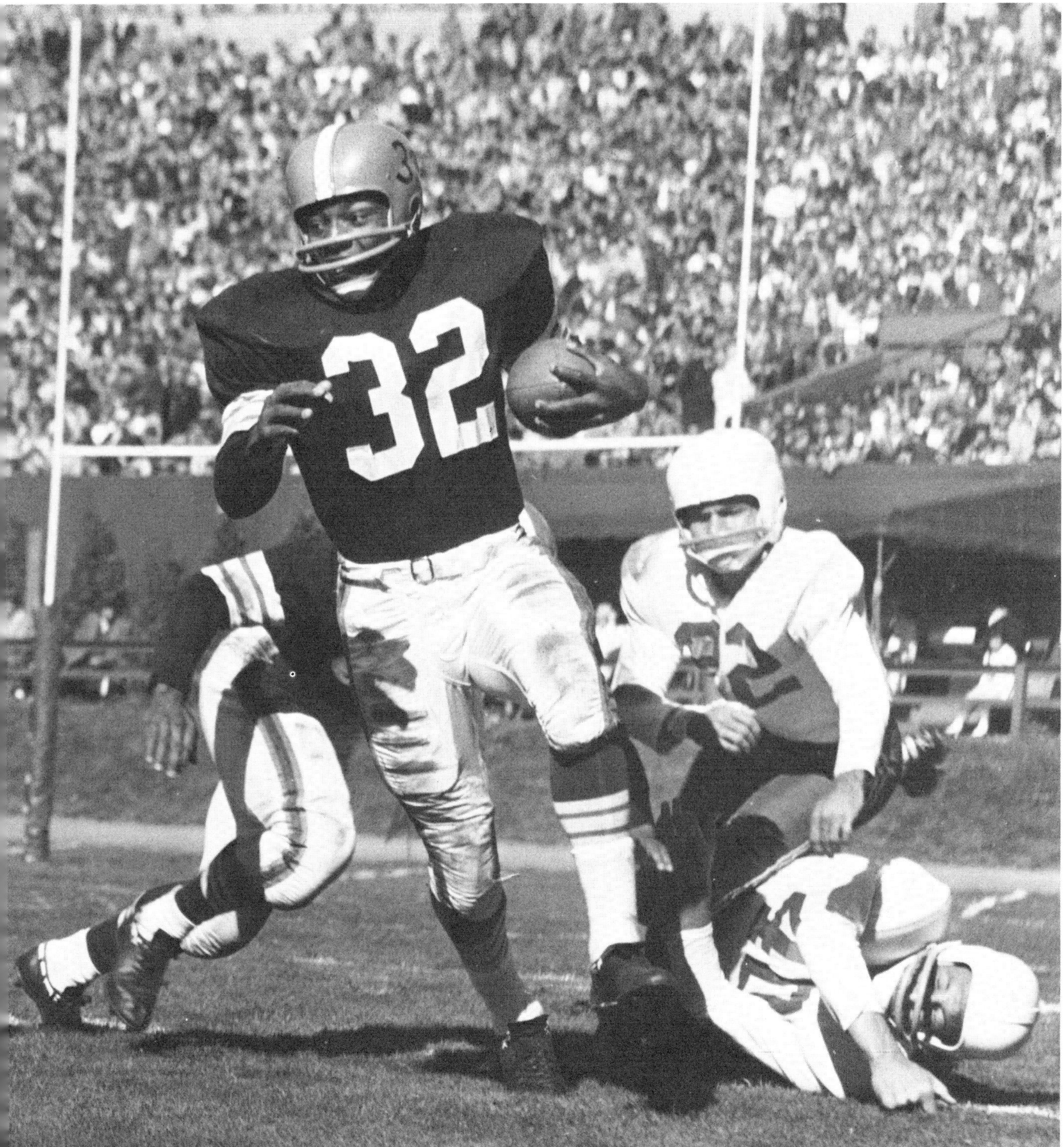

In 1961, Brown established another record by rushing 305 times during the season. In 1962, Brown injured his arm and failed to win the rushing title for the first and only time in his nine-year career. But the following season, twenty-seven-year-old Brown came back with a fury and rushed for 1,863 yards. For his efforts, Brown signed a contract worth $65,000 a year.

In 1964, Brown played in his first championship game. He rushed for 114 yards as the Browns beat the Baltimore Colts 27-0. In 1965, Brown rushed for 1,544 yards.

The handsome, athletic superstar was getting endorsement offers from everywhere. Even Hollywood wanted Jim Brown to star in movies for them. The movie offer was tempting. In Hollywood, Brown could make more money than he could playing football. And the work would be a lot easier on his body. Brown decided to become an actor.

Before the 1966 season, Jim Brown announced his retirement from football. The fans thought he was holding out for more money. But Brown meant what he said and left football at the height of his career.

Jim Brown was the greatest running back of all-time.

Upon his retirement after nine seasons, Jim Brown had established himself as the greatest halfback in professional football history. He had led the league in rushing eight times, he had gained the most yards in a season (1,863), he had rushed for the most yards in a career (12,312), he had the highest rushing average (5.22), and he had scored the most touchdowns (126).

For his remarkable accomplishments, Jim Brown was elected into the Pro Football Hall of Fame in 1971. Had he played longer, Jim Brown probably would have established records that no one could have broken.